Dear Father,

I thank you for all your work through me that your name will be glorified.

I pray that many will know Jesus is Your Son, and that He came to save.

May Your work shine forever..

In Christ,

Lewis Satini

Once there was
A SHEPHERD

Who owned hundreds of sheep
AND KNEW EACH OF
THEIR NAMES

EVERY MORNING
HE BROUGHT THE SHEEP WHERE
THE GRASS WAS
GREEN

AND BEFORE THE DAWN,
HE TOOK THEM BACK
TO THE SAFETY OF
THEIR HOME.

WHILE WALKING,

HE COUNTED THEM AND CALLED
THEM BY NAME TO BE SURE NOT
ONE WAS MISSING.

ONE EVENING,
HE COUNTED THEM AND
CALLED THEIR NAMES.

HE CALLED
"ONE".

THEN
"TWO".

HE CALLED
"THREE".

THEN
"FOUR".

WHEN HE CALLED "FIVE",
THERE WAS NO RESPONSE.
HE WAS NOWHERE
TO BE FOUND NEAR THE GROUP.

WITHOUT A SECOND THOUGHT,

HE IMMEDIATELY LEFT HUNDREDS OF SHEEP
TO GO AND FIND "FIVE" THE LOST SHEEP.

HE LOOKED EVERYWHERE,

He even went to the lost and found office, but there was no report of a sheep that lost its way.

THEN HE WENT AGAIN

AND ASKED

SOME BIRDS, IF THEY
HAD SEEN "FIVE"
SHEEP, BUT THEY
MERELY IGNORED HIM.

THE NIGHT
HAD FALLEN,

BUT STILL "FIVE" WAS
NOWHERE TO BE FOUND.

HE THOUGHT ABOUT "FIVE"
AND WORRIED ALL NIGHT.

WHAT IF HE HAS NO SHELTER?
WHAT IF NO ONE GIVES HIM
FOOD? WHAT IF HE HAS NO ONE
TO GUIDE HIM HOME?

HE THOUGHT ABOUT
WHERE "FIVE" MIGHT BE?
WHERE WAS HIS FAVORITE
PLACE TO GO?

SUDDENLY,

THOUGHT

CAME TO HIS MIND.

HE QUICKLY RAN

TO THAT PLACE AND
LOOKED FOR HIM.

HE LOOKED
FOR HOURS.

AT LAST,
HE FOUND THE SHEEP.

THE SHEEP
WAS VERY SCARED.

HE HELD HIM TIGHT
WITH A JOYFUL HEART
AND CARRIED HIM BACK
TO JOIN THE GROUP.

HE WAS SO HAPPY
THAT HE GATHERED
ALL HIS FAMILY AND FRIENDS.

AND SAID

"COME AND
CELEBRATE WITH ME,
FOR I HAVE FOUND
MY LOST SHEEP..."

HE WAS FILLED WITH MORE *Joy*
OVER THAT ONE WHO WAS LOST
BUT CAME BACK TO HIM
THAN OVER ALL THE REST
WHO WERE ALREADY SAVED.

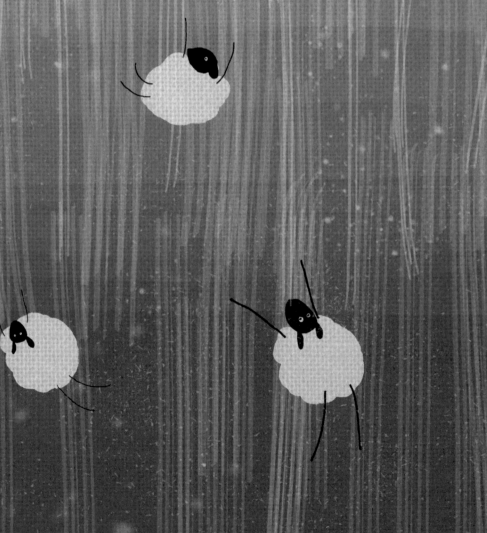

Born Lewis Satini on January 17,1979, in Medan, Indonesia. Lewis Satini is an illustrator and designer.

Lewis Satini earned a BFA in Computer Animation from Academy of Art University. As an illustrator and designer, he is well-versed in myriad traditional and digital media.

Lewis Satini has published "Planting A Kingdom Seed" (2014), "The Wise Koala" (2014) and "Lost and Found" (2017).

Lewis Satini was inspired by the life of Jesus Christ. As a follower of Jesus Christ, he wish the story to reflect the very basis of the life of Christianity and that the story glorifies His Name and His beautiful creation. He wish that all the children around the nations will know the story of Jesus Christ.

facebook.com/lewis.satini
jubilee.lewis@gmail.com

Made in the USA
San Bernardino, CA
23 January 2020